C000157408

What's On Top?

Co-Counselling:
what is it and why
would I want to do it?

Steve Roche & Sue Gray

What's On Top?

Co-Counselling:
what is it and why
would I want to do it?

"Listening is a magnetic and strange thing,
a creative force. The friends who listen
to us are the ones we move toward.
When we are listened to, it creates us,
makes us unfold and expand."

- *Karl A. Menninger*

CONTENTS

INTRODUCTION

While running trainings and tasters we are often asked, 'Is there anything I can read?'. In speaking to friends, colleagues and professionals about co-counselling, we frequently encounter confusion and mistaken assumptions about what it is.

The same range of questions get asked, including an implicit one about how co-counselling can compete alongside the plethora of self-development methods available. There are several excellent full-scale manuals that support co-counselling training, but no short and readable introduction to the subject.

We produced this book to address all these needs. In the process of working out exactly what it is, why we do it and in what ways it is useful, we discovered other motivations - such as the desire to clarify our own thinking, and our own assessment of the value and relevance of co-counselling in the 21st century.

There is also a desire to stimulate debate which might perhaps prompt some development of thought. We appreciate that this work is one perspective, that others in the co-counselling community may see things differently.

We have come to a greater appreciation of the power of co-counselling as an entry into self-awareness and the journey of self-development. Also as a source of tools that empower people to build emotional literacy and to create a satisfying and fulfilling life for themselves and with the people around them.

Why the title?

"What's On Top?" is a question used in co-counselling. It asks what in the moment is uppermost in conscious thought for the client. It is an invitation to articulate this without necessarily making sense, and a useful way to begin a session. Giving free reign to conscious thoughts gives the unconscious the chance to emerge. It helps the person to become present in the moment and to connect with their body and feelings.

1. What Is It?

What is this book?

A concise and readable introduction to co-counselling that answers these questions:

- Why is it important to learn about the impact my emotions have on me?
- How will a better understanding of my emotions improve and enrich my life?
- How can co-counselling help me make the changes I want?
- What makes it different from other ways of working, and how do I know if it's right for me?

Who is it for?

People who want to know more about co-counselling, and about the skills of managing their emotional states. That includes people who:

- Enjoy learning new things and want to explore their inner world
- Want to develop their emotional intelligence
- Want to connect with like-minded people who share similar values
- Want a way to support themselves and to work on their own issues
- Are looking to create an emotional support network
- Are looking for self-development tools or life skills to supplement their practice
- Seek an accessible and low-cost way to get into counselling
- Want to move on from doing one-way therapy or counselling.

But it's also for people who've never heard of co-counselling, but who just:

- Have problems they don't know how to deal with

- Need better ways to cope with life and work

- Want a system or process that will help them make effective changes.

How will it help?

Once you've read the book you should understand:

- What co-counselling is, and how it differs from other approaches
- How and why it works
- What sort of people use it, and what they get from it
- How to learn co-counselling and use it in your life
- What benefits you can expect from becoming a co-counsellor.

Scope

1. Although much of the book is relevant to an international readership, it is written for a UK audience.
2. It is an introductory text, that makes no attempt to explain everything fully. It is definitely not an alternative to a formal training in co-counselling.
3. It is solely about **co**-counselling. It is not about becoming a professional practitioner (although the co-counselling skills are relevant and useful to anyone working as therapist, counsellor or coach).
4. It is one view of co-counselling as expressed by one teaching team. We expect there to be many additional and alternative viewpoints ☺
5. The scope is deliberately limited for this first version. The book will be updated periodically on the basis of feedback received.
6. It is about co-counselling in the context of CCI (Co-Counselling International) and does not attempt to address RC (Re-evaluation Counselling).

How to use the book

Dip in and out, skip anything that doesn't interest you, and use the bits that are helpful. Most of the words in bold are explained in the Glossary.

We like feedback! So please tell us what worked well for you, what should be done differently or what you'd like more of. Contact information is in Section 16.

Steve Roche and Sue Gray

2. Why Is It Needed?

How are emotions sometimes unhelpful?

Feelings sometimes arise unexpectedly and stop us doing what we want to do or being who we want to be. Have you ever thought after an event or an exchange: 'Why did I do that again?', 'That's not what I really wanted', 'Why does X get one over on me so often?', 'I was behaving like a kid'.

Probably what happened is that just before the event or exchange some other experience happened that 'triggered' a feeling in you. This emotional reaction was linked in some way to a past experience (often in childhood). It caused you to behave in the same way in the present as you would have done in the past.

Sometimes this means that you behave in an 'out of date' way. It's a bit like using a modern instruction manual for an outdated machine. Or finding your software no longer works properly because you haven't upgraded to the latest version.

How do unhelpful emotions get created?

Feelings are often useful and important. They are part of being human – and they enable us to learn, change and grow. Emotional reactions can also protect us and keep us safe. But like other resources or abilities, they need to be understood and used carefully. Rather than the 'tail wagging the dog', it's about the tail and the dog working together to create balance, harmony, awareness and change.

We all have basic physical needs - for food, drink, sleep, warmth, shelter. We also have psychological and emotional needs, which include to love and be loved (meaning the capacity to care and be cared for; to be concerned for each other); to understand and be understood; to live by our own values and beliefs; to be free to live with other people who are doing the same.

What happens when these needs are not met?

We grieve when we don't receive love, we are frightened when we don't feel understood, we are angry and frustrated when we cannot be free and self-directed (living by our own values and beliefs).

When these needs are not met, we experience certain distressed responses. As a result, we start behaving and believing in certain ways which at the time seem - and often are - appropriate ways to respond. But time moves on and our situation and abilities change. Those beliefs and behaviours were for *then* and they don't work *now* - or sometimes are not needed now.

When emotions from the past create behaviours that are out of date, we get 'tripped up' by them. Then we don't have access to all of our abilities and resources because our attention and energy is focussed in a different place.

It's a bit like a computer that gets infected with a virus. It suddenly slows down because in the background it's working hard to deal with a problem and therefore doesn't have sufficient memory to run the current task at a proper speed. At worst, the whole computer crashes and does not work at all. Sometimes that happens to people.

We feel distressed and unhappy when our basic needs are not met. Sometimes we are not consciously aware of such distress: sometimes our bodies feel the feeling but our head does not.

All **emotions** have a bodily expression – we cry when we are sad, laugh when we are happy, shake when we are frightened, blush when we are embarrassed. To be emotional most effectively we need to express feelings physically as well as in our heads. When we are able to do that, we avoid building up emotional baggage.

Why do we tell ourselves unhelpful things?

Most of us remember hearing things like, 'I wouldn't do that, it will never work'... 'You must do this or else'... 'You shouldn't do that'... These messages bombard us throughout childhood – you should / ought / must be other than you are. These shoulds and oughts and musts are other people's rules being imposed on us, often in an unhelpful way.

We often take other people's **beliefs**, **values** and rules inside and adopt them as our own rules for life. They become our truths, seeming to show us the right and wrong in every situation. We believe this is the only truth about how things are, and other people need to behave this way too, or else!

One long-term effect of these messages is that we become unsure whether we are doing the right thing, frequently needing the approval of other people before we feel OK. If we become dependent on that approval to function, the result is low **self-esteem** (not valuing ourselves) and an inability to make decisions. The outcome is frequently an ill-defined frustration or dissatisfaction with the way our lives are working out.

How does this relate to the life we lead now?

Feelings impact on our behaviour. When unhelpful feelings arise from a reaction to the past (including shoulds and oughts), that stops us being authentic in the present. Bringing our understanding and awareness to this over time frees us to reach our full potential and live more authentically from our own beliefs and values. Then we can be happier and more satisfied with our lives, and therefore be more connected, compassionate and useful to the people around us. The result is that we feel more fully alive.

3. How Does It Help?

How can co-counselling skills and techniques help?

Our experiences, messages, beliefs and feelings get stored in our bodies as well as our minds. Storing unhelpful experiences is harmful. To avoid the impact of holding on to things in our bodies that do not help us, we need to express them and to let them go.

The **interventions** taught in co-counselling help us to find our emotions and feel them, then to **discharge** and process the unhelpful ones. This changes the emotions so that they don't interfere with what we want to do in a way that causes us problems.

The co-counselling techniques and **framework** help us to recognise past hurts and old messages. With the support built into the process, it then feels safe enough in the present to express and let go of past experiences that are not useful. A release of emotional tension that frees up our energy and restores our spirits in this way is known as **catharsis** - and it can happen in many different ways.

After discharge or catharsis we often feel more energised. This is because holding on to unhelpful emotions - keeping them stuffed down or suppressed – uses up our energy. When we stop holding on, the energy is released for other things – a bit like unblocking a pipe and suddenly restoring the flow.

Holding down unhelpful emotions or running a lot on other people's rules can be a contributory factor in many illnesses, such as gastric conditions, arthritis, depression and M.E.

In a co-counselling session we use the techniques to get us to a place where we can let go of unhelpful **patterns** that were imprinted in our minds and bodies from past experiences. Then we can more efficiently sort out problems as they arise, as if we had a new 'manual' that was up-to-date and easy to follow.

Patterns

A pattern is a repetitive piece of behaviour resulting from an old stimulus, where the same trigger gets the same response. Some people think of it as getting their 'buttons pressed'. An example – you were teased when a child about being lazy and you became very sensitive about it. As a result, you probably work very hard most of your life to disprove it. Not only that, but every time someone makes a remark that might imply you are not pulling your weight – however harmless the intention – you react badly and appear defensive or hit back. Someone doing this is reacting from a pattern rather than acting as an emotionally healthy adult.

How can we 'fix' a pattern?

Co-counselling can give us the skills for gathering information about what we are doing that is a patterned reaction, both emotional and physical. It's a bit like a computer running an outdated programme, or a CD that is scratched and gets stuck or 'jumps' when that part of it is played. As you collect information related to the situation, you can let go of it, understand more about it, and see how you could 're-programme' yourself to deal with it differently.

How does it work?

Co-counselling offers both a framework and a culture. These give us the safety to use the techniques to explore our 'emotional landscape'. With a better understanding of how this landscape was created, we can see more clearly how we hold ourselves back, and learn to deal more effectively with routine events in our lives. Re-connecting with experiences in our past helps us see how they created the feelings and beliefs we have now – and how they drive our responses to what happens in the present.

Within the safety and support of a co-counselling session we get to feel those emotions and bodily sensations again, and to express them in a more useful and healing way, as we are freed up from the restrictions of our past experiences. This is how **emotional intelligence** develops... we understand our emotions more fully as they get integrated more effectively into who we are: we gain insight and can optimise our healthy and empowered selves.

Having cleared out the things that have been holding us back, we can **re-evaluate** the situation and understand more clearly what needs doing next. Then we can plan to make it happen in a way we will be able to achieve. (See **Action Setting** in Section 9.)

Why might we not have expressed emotions healthily?

As children we are often prevented from expressing feelings that are entirely appropriate at the time. If you watch a child trip and fall, their natural and healthy response is to be upset, to cry and run for comfort. If they receive comfort and their hurt is acknowledged, they quickly go from being distressed to jumping up and running off to play happily again as if nothing had happened.

An emotionally healthy adult would acknowledge the hurt and allow a child to discharge the distress. But this often doesn't happen. That's firstly because of social norms, like "it's not OK to express emotion... boys don't cry... girls don't get angry... it's selfish to ask for what you need... don't blow your own trumpet."

The second reason is that we don't like to watch someone in distress: it's painful and it reminds us of our own distress. This is why people often try to block expression of emotion in others, saying things like 'be a brave little soldier',' don't be so silly', 'pull yourself together and get on with it'. As children (and adults) we want to please and to be liked, so we quickly conform to the 'norm' or accept the message, suppressing what we would do naturally. We forget that as human beings we are designed to have emotions and to express them safely and appropriately. To do so allows us to be strong and resourceful.

How past hurts can affect present behaviour

Examples of what people may do when driven by unmet needs or shoulds and oughts:

- Act unassertively with people in authority because they were frightened by authority figures (e.g. headmaster, doctor) as a child.
- Have sex when they don't really want to, as a way to feel loved and connected.
- Interrupt a lot and not listen, because they were not listened to or given space to talk as a child.

- Stay in a toxic relationship because they learned that you marry for life and it's not OK to get divorced.
- Act angrily and aggressively because they feel frightened and unsafe, and being angry keeps people away.
- Lack compassion and tenderness, having been told that it was weak and pathetic.
- Behave disruptively, trying to get the care and attention they didn't get as a child.
- End relationships as soon as they become close and intimate.
- Always get ill at holiday times because they find it difficult to rest and to take care of themselves.

Doing it differently

There is a co-counselling technique that is used to take you back to a key event in the *past* which is having a negative impact on the way you want to be in the *present*. It allows you to re-run the experience in a more helpful way, which brings clarity and healing. This is often followed by new insight and understanding.

Once you can see new ways of doing things, you can choose to live in a different way and plan the actions to make it happen. Towards the end of a co-counselling session, following re-evaluation, there is a process of decision-making around your new-found values and beliefs. (See Action Setting in Section 9). From this new place you can construct a stronger and more sustainable identity. You can update your database, renew your instruction manual, upgrade your software, and release more disc space!

Summary

We have basic human needs that are not always met appropriately in impressionable childhood. We create patterns or 'workarounds' to deal with this. Some of these are not helpful, and as time passes they become blocks to us living a full and satisfying life.

Co-counselling provides a set of tools within a framework to assist in identifying the unhelpful things we have learned in the past – a bit like updating the obsolete manual – so we can re-programme and set new directions. Then we can deal more effectively with life, maintain our emotional health and create a happier and more satisfying future.

"The sharing of hurt is the beginning of healing"
– *Archbishop Robert Runcie*

4. Is It For Me?

Co-counselling is a method for increasing emotional intelligence and supporting individual growth. It provides a way to discover, express and manage feelings, to plan actions and outcomes, and to learn more about ourselves. It offers a network of like-minded people who can become a personal, social and emotional support system for life. It is a great way of maintaining good mental health.

In contrast to traditional counselling:

- It is always self-directed: the client is totally in charge of their own work and their own **balance of attention**.
- It is reciprocal: based on an equal exchange of time, skills and attention, with half the time spent as 'talker' and half as 'listener'.

- It's free for life: after the initial training, you never pay for another session of co-counselling.
- The basics can be learnt in a relatively short time – usually 40 hours – with no previous experience of this type of work.

Co-counselling is not a professional training. It won't teach you the skills to become a professional counsellor and charge for your time and expertise. But if one of your objectives is to earn a living as a counsellor or psychotherapist, a training in co-counselling will certainly help you on your way. You will have created a valuable network and gained a lot of useful skills. You will have a better understanding of yourself - how your emotional anatomy works, how you can live with your feelings and not have them run your life.

Who uses co-counselling?

People who want to explore their inner world, within a personal support network... who want to learn self-development tools and life skills to grow their emotional intelligence. A number of co-counsellors are 'skilled helpers', working in areas like teaching, coaching, facilitation, management, and therapy - they learn valuable skills from co-counselling and get valuable support from it. Many others just enjoy and appreciate it as part of their lives, friendships and personal or social support system.

What is co-counselling for?

We may notice ourselves doing something and afterwards wonder 'Why did I do that?' Or:

- we notice that we'd *like* to do it but there's something stopping us
- we want to explore whether we could enjoy life more, or deal with it better
- we do a job that is emotionally and psychologically challenging
- we may feel like somebody else is driving our life, not us
- we have feelings that often overwhelm, confuse, or frighten us

- we have feelings that seem inappropriate, or feel like they don't belong to us
- we don't feel anything at all, and that seems odd
- our relationships keep on causing us trouble
- we often feel like we don't fit in, or feel shy or awkward, or don't seem to be able to get on with people.

If you identify something like this that is affecting your life in a way you don't want, you may decide you need to find out more about it, to change it, and create a plan of action to do something different. Co-counselling is one way you can do that. We can refer to these things as the 'work', the 'material', the 'issue', or just our 'stuff'.

Co-counselling for maintenance

If you think of your car, or your computer, or even your body:

- Sometimes it breaks down and needs fixing quickly.

- It may be running quite well, but there's a rattle, squeak or intermittent fault.
- There may be nothing wrong, but you know you must service and maintain it to keep it in good order.

he co-counselling equivalent is 'emotional maintenance'. Here are some scenarios:

- You are doing well in one area of your life but have challenges in others (e.g. You're successful at work but can't keep a relationship going... You put all your energy into raising a family and now are frustrated in your career... After a long time in one relationship you're suddenly on your own).
- You want some way of giving yourself emotional 'space' – for reflecting, sharing or emoting in a supported and safe way.
- You are doing OK generally, it's just that you want to live life more fully and learn to deal more skilfully with the ups and downs.

- You suddenly feel emotional in a way that's unexpected or unwelcome.
- You receive distressing or puzzling feedback.
- You have trouble with certain sorts of people.
- You work in a highly-charged or emotionally challenging environment. The stress puts extra demands on your resources, so you need to recharge and recuperate. You need a way to process and let go of the impact of work so as not to carry 'baggage' from it into the rest of your life.

Co-counselling can help in all of these situations by providing a space to explore our reactions and feelings, then to express and accept them, leading on to understanding and change. The mechanism is the release of emotional and physical tension followed by insight and healing. We explain what we mean by this in other parts of the book.

How does this work?

This system of personal change and growth works by addressing universal human needs and drivers. It gives you a framework and a structure, but also flexibility and choice to do what you need to do in your own way. It builds on your own inherent strengths and resources. We have all survived and got this far in life, so we all have useful life experience, have learned ways of getting through things, and have accumulated significant skills and knowledge.

Co-counselling presupposes that you can take your present experience, knowledge and capabilities, and use them more skilfully to help you feel better, move forward and stay emotionally healthy. It's not a case of something from outside being put into you, but rather what you have inside being brought out. Then you can use it in new and more powerful ways to live a happier and richer life.

What do people get from it?

At first it's about learning ways of approaching things a little differently in order to feel a little bit better. If you go on using it consistently you become more and more skilled and continue to build your emotional intelligence. Over time, it's a way to become happier and more peaceful, and feel like a more capable human being. The biggest benefits are:

1. Confidence – feeling more confident at work, at home, in groups, and in your family.

2. Boundaries – knowing and choosing where your personal boundaries are and what that means for you.

3. Self-Knowledge - an increased awareness and understanding of yourself. A greater ability to be fully present and in the moment.

4. Personal Healing and Growth - understanding and dealing with the effects of past traumas and hurts, so that your past no longer limits your present and your future.

5. Better Relationships – with colleagues, families, partners, children, in groups. Learning to communicate better to create and maintain relationships that enrich your life rather than limit it.

6. Handling Life – more options, choices and flexibility, so you are able to decide how to react to what life presents you with.

7. Social Networks – creating meaningful connections and friendships with like-minded people.

8. Fun – it's not all about dealing with deep and dark problems. Sessions can be tough, but there's often a reaction of joy and pleasure and a feeling of lightness that follows the release of emotional 'baggage'. Co-counselling events – evenings, days, weekends and weeks – include a lot of laughter and fun. Many people meet partners and make lifelong friendships through co-counselling.

Achieving emotional balance

If we close down emotionally, we avoid the bad feelings but we don't get the good feelings either. Most people find that co-counselling offers a way to discover and release new parts of themselves they didn't even know about.

5. What's The Culture?

It's true that co-counselling is 'counter-cultural' in some ways – it's not what people 'normally' do, so it will often feel unfamiliar and strange at first. Here we address some common reactions.

1. 'It's weird to talk about your feelings'
Although it's much more acceptable for people to show emotions (e.g. for men to cry), change is slow, and there's still a lot of discomfort about sharing emotion in public. It is perhaps a particular problem for the English, with our persistent cultural norms and legacy of Victorian values and stiff upper lips.

But our emotions are helpful and important, and a normal part of being human. We need to understand and handle them effectively. Co-counselling is a self-development tool that provides a framework for learning about and working with emotions.

People who manage their emotions well are more successful in all areas of life. Analysis of what makes successful people tick shows that it's far less about conventional intelligence (having a high IQ), and far more about *emotional* intelligence (having a high EQ). Co-counselling teaches people to be more emotionally intelligent.

2. 'It's weird to show off and boast'

There is an emphasis on **celebration** in co-counselling which is similarly counter-cultural. At first, most of us find that being invited to celebrate ourselves and be celebrated by others feels strange. It may seem awkward or embarrassing, and our self-talk goes into overdrive with dire warnings about being smug and blowing our own trumpet. But we can learn to appreciate having the freedom to counter unhelpful childhood messages about how bad it is to show off.

Celebration is a direct connection to our inner resources. We have all done things well and we all have things to celebrate – even though it's sometimes hard to find them, feel good about them and realise their value. The more you do it the easier and more natural it becomes. Better still, most people's experience is that it leads to permanent growth. Research shows that our bodies change physically when we allow ourselves to feel good, that actually strengthens our immune systems. A helpful book on this subject is "The Endorphin Effect" by William Bloom.

'It's weird to talk to strangers about personal things'

We might expect it to be easier to talk to others about personal things when we know each other well. But what really happens when we talk to friends and family? They may make assumptions, they don't always listen well, they tend to give advice based on what would work for them, or even tell us what to do. Family members may treat us in familiar and well-worn ways based on unhelpful patterns laid down long ago – because it is hard for all of us to change our roles in the family.

Co-counselling allows you to be listened to without interruption. The structure reduces the impact of other people's agendas, as you are supported to come up with your own solution based on your own resources.

Why is it good to talk to 'strangers'?

Co-counselling is about building your own resources and running your own inner life, becoming more independent, self-reliant and self-directed. Talking to someone who does not know you well is much more likely to broaden your perspective and increase your options. Life is not simple, so the more options you have, the better. It's always good to have a variety of solutions. It's a scientific principle that in any system the most successful organism is that which displays the greatest behavioural flexibility

People who know us well are often not so good at helping us increase our options. It's more effective to do that with someone who is objective and impartial and not running their own agenda. We are often held back from doing what we want to do by trying to please the very people to whom we go for support. We need to enjoy friends and family, but not live to please them.

"There is an expiry date on blaming your parents
for steering you in the wrong direction;
the moment you are old enough to take the wheel,
responsibility lies with you."

– *J. K. Rowling*

6. How Do I Learn It?

How do people learn co-counselling?

The basic requirement for becoming a co-counsellor is to undergo a 'Fundamentals' training. These courses are run throughout the year at various locations in the UK. If you want to sign up for a training you simply need to choose your area and contact the relevant teacher.

If you are not sure yet about committing to a Fundamentals, you will usually be able to attend a taster event (below) or at least to meet up with a local teacher to discuss the training and get your questions answered.

There is helpful information about trainings and teachers on the CCI (UK) website (see 'Further Information').

It may be that there is nothing suitable in or around your area, or that you just want to talk to someone generally about co-counselling. The website also shows a list of 'contact people' by county, which you can use to identify the appropriate person to get in touch with.

Fundamentals training

In order to become accredited as a co-counsellor and be invited to join the co-counselling community, every individual is required to undertake a basic training known as Fundamentals of Co-counselling.

The training is a minimum of forty hours and may be offered in several different formats - for example as a series of evenings and weekends, or as weekly classes maybe at an adult education institution. Usually the training is spread over five full days, typically two weekends and an extra day. Often these weekends are a couple of weeks apart, which makes arrangements easier and allows for people to absorb and practise what they have learned in between.

The training is highly experiential, with the emphasis on doing rather than just listening. So although you may take notes and absorb information, it is not simply about learning theory in an abstract way. Instead a new idea or technique is presented, demonstrated and discussed, then an exercise is undertaken to give everyone the opportunity to try it out. The main learning is in the personal experience.

People work in pairs, in smaller groups or in the whole group, following the pattern of learn a little bit, try it out, give feedback, learn from others, ask questions, share personal experiences, exchange feedback. Often the Fundamentals course ends with an accreditation process (see below), where the emphasis is mainly on the demonstration of the basic skills rather than a knowledge of theory, technique and terminology.

Tasters

A number of teachers offer what they call 'taster' events. These typically run for a couple of hours in an evening or weekend so it's easier for people to get there. The taster is a low-risk way to try out co-counselling and see if you like it, without committing yourself.

If you go to a taster session you'll meet other people who are interested in doing the training. You also get a chance to meet your teacher(s), and perhaps some other experienced members of the community. There will be a few exercises and demonstrations designed to help you get a feel for how co-counselling works, and to assess whether it is going to appeal to you personally. You get to hear about community activities and see how they might work for you.

The advantage of attending a taster is that you can ask all the questions you want. You can also find out practical information about such things as costs, dates, times, accommodation and venue, and understand what kind of commitment you would be making. But you'll also get a feel for what it is and whether it suits you, and if it feels like your kind of thing. Then you will be in a position to make an informed decision about your future with co-counselling.

After Fundamentals

The Fundamentals is the only training you are required to undertake in order to become a co-counsellor and to join the community. Some people see their fundamentals course as a bit like passing the driving test: you are fully qualified to practise, yet in a way you are only just beginning to learn. And it may be quite some time before you feel really confident and experienced, and able to handle any situation.

So what sort of things help to build this sense of confidence? The main thing is to do lots of sessions, as you will gain experience every time you work. Sometimes you will get helpful feedback, and often you get the chance to pick up ideas from what your partner does. Working with a range of different co-counsellors is an excellent way to learn about other people's approaches and to see how they interpret and apply the interventions in different ways.

Another good way of developing and expanding your co-counselling skills is through workshops and group activities. These typically happen at community events (which usually run for a day or an evening) and at residential events (which vary in length from a long weekend to a week).

For example, one of the things you might discover is that although the basic form of co-counselling is working in pairs, some people also like to work in threes or larger groups. The longer workshops give you the chance to try out this way of working, and even if it does not appeal to you personally, it is worth allowing yourself a different experience. It's often helpful to try new things in unfamiliar formats to help develop not only our skills but also our understanding of ourselves and others.

Is there a standard syllabus of interventions?

There is a set of CCI co-counselling interventions that might be thought of as 'standard', although in practice the exact set taught will depend on the particular teachers. Each Fundamentals teacher has developed their training around the core co-counselling principles together with their own adaptations and interpretations. This core set is documented in the training manuals used and produced by the people who are currently teaching.

What each person learns gives them enough common understanding of the culture and interventions to ensure that whenever they meet a CCI co-counsellor from any country they will be able to co-counsel together.

Maintaining standards

CCI co-counselling in the UK is not regulated or administered by any central body. In practice the community regulates what is being taught, which means that 'quality control' is a shared responsibility.

There will be an awareness in the community of teaching activity and an informal monitoring of people graduating from fundamentals courses. As newer co-counsellors mix and work with those who are more experienced, an inevitable levelling and integration follows.

Most teachers also enlist the support of experienced co-counsellors to participate and assist on fundamentals courses. They are usually known as 'helpers', or sometimes 'participant observers'. Their presence enriches the student's experience and ensures a variety of input and a continuing cross-fertilisation of ideas – as well as being another way to monitor and maintain standards.

Many teachers have attended a co-counselling teacher training event and been specifically accredited to teach the Fundamentals of Co-counselling course. Potential teachers also learn by helping and working alongside experienced teachers.

Accreditation

At the end of a Fundamentals training most teachers run an accreditation process. The aim of this is to assess each individual's suitability to join the CCI community.

In keeping with the principles of co-counselling, accreditation is the responsibility of the whole group: it is not about being assessed or marked solely by the teachers. Everyone present has responsibility for giving feedback on each other person on the course, specifically in regard to their ability to deliver on the basic skills and to adhere to co-counselling rules and guidelines.

Typically, each individual assesses their own level of skill and their suitability to be accredited as a co-counsellor, perhaps also noting their strengths and their areas for improvement. Every other person present gives their opinion as to whether that person is ready to be accredited, and may also add any comments about what they do particularly well and what they need to develop.

Following successful accreditation, each participant is welcomed into the co-counselling community. They will be put in touch with local co-counsellors, given access to email lists and websites, and encouraged to attend as many future events as they wish.

Further development

Some co-counselling events focus specifically on developing current skills or introducing additional ones. This often happens at residential events where people offer a theory or try out a new technique at a workshop. This may or may not lead to anything, but occasionally a new approach emerges which adds to the existing body of knowledge and practice. However, there is always a concern to keep within the spirit and original concept of CCI co-counselling, and not to change it into something that would no longer be recognised by co-counsellors all over the world.

There may also be specific Further Skills events, which are dedicated to learning and improving existing co-counselling skills and finding ways to use them more effectively.

"Perhaps once in a hundred years a person may be ruined by excessive praise, but surely once every minute someone dies inside for lack of it."

- Cecil G. Osborne

7. Can I Do It At Work?

Can co-counselling be taught at work?

The skills and awareness that co-counselling teaches are useful in all walks of life, including work, and can become a valuable part of a staff support system. Modified versions of co-counselling have been successfully taught in hospital settings to nursing, therapy, medical and administration staff, and also to volunteers and staff within local authorities.

In these settings the training is more usually known as 'Peer Staff Support'. It helps people create a safe and confidential way to discuss issues that come up at work. The basic principles and skills of co-counselling are taught along with a framework for group and two-way support and supervision sessions, tailored to the needs of the organisation.

If participants in Peer Staff Support trainings wish to become full co-counsellors, they complete a further day which includes additional skills practice and accreditations. This satisfies the CCI requirement for forty hours training.

What are the benefits of co-counselling in the workplace?

"Emotional intelligence is not a luxury
you can dispense with in tough times.
It's a basic tool that, deployed with finesse,
is the key to professional success."

- *Harvard Business School Review*

Success at work has a lot to do with how we relate to the people around us and how we appear to them. The skills and tools learned in co-counselling are hugely beneficial in all types of relationship. At work they will help you to develop emotional intelligence and greatly increase your understanding of yourself, your colleagues, managers, and people who report to you.

Increased emotional intelligence is a recognised way to be more successful at work. Greater self-assurance and effectiveness improves perceived value in many ways. Skills learned in co-counselling training that are relevant to work, include how to:

- Give clear and effective feedback
- Be more resourceful when imparting bad news
- Get on at work even when feeling upset; avoid getting 'stuck' in feelings
- Use fun and lightness at work to increase effectiveness
- Relate openly and honestly to people
- Increase people's willingness to work together and be more productive
- Be more assertive and self-responsible
- Listen and question more effectively

- Build rapport and get along with colleagues better
- Improve skill at 'managing upwards'
- Handle conflict well and put useful boundaries in place
- Appreciate people and trust them to use their own resources.

8. What Happens In A Session?

How is a co-counselling session set up?

The basic idea is that one person talks while the other person listens, and then they swap over. The one who talks first is the **client**; the one who listens first is the **counsellor**. When they swap over, the client becomes counsellor and the counsellor becomes client.

When two people meet for a session they decide who will be client first. They also decide how long the sessions will be. Both people always have the same length of time. So if the total time available is fifty minutes, they may decide to have twenty minutes session time each, which allows ten minutes for everything else (including time between sessions to change roles and give feedback). An electronic timer is often used to help keep track of time.

The person who is being client decides what they want to talk about. It is a fundamental principle that the client always chooses their material and is in charge of their own session.

The client also chooses the way they want to work, by selecting a particular **contract**. There are three contracts in co-counselling: Free Attention contract, Normal contract, Intensive contract.

Whichever contract is requested, the main job of the counsellor is to listen attentively. The ability to give good attention is the basic requirement of co-counselling, and the most important skill learned on Fundamentals training.

Free Attention contract

This is a truly valuable skill to learn, and one which can be used in many aspects of life to great benefit. The skill is *active silent listening.* It is a gift that you give someone when you are their counsellor. The client is in charge: this is their time to do whatever they choose. As counsellor your job is to listen and witness in a totally non-judgemental way. You are actively listening: not thinking about lunch or planning what you'd do to solve their problem for them!

Free Attention consists of giving your full awareness to the client, looking at them so that if they look up and want eye contact with you, it will be there and they can have it. You avoid giving any facial expression, body movement, touch or words to the client. Any of these may influence their material and affect the direction of their work.

Free Attention needs to be practised - it feels odd to give and to receive when you first start doing it.

This feeling reduces as you get used to it and see and feel the benefit of active silent listening. Free attention listening is an important part of what allows the client to be solely responsible for their own work. When in doubt as a counsellor you can and should always return to the free attention contract. Sometimes it is all that's needed to allow your client to have a productive session.

Normal contract

When a Normal contract has been specified, the counsellor may offer one or more of the specific co-counselling **interventions** during the session. An intervention is offered to the client with the intention of helping them to progress with their work. There are a few examples in the sample dialogue in Section 9.

The counsellor may 'intervene' by offering a question or suggestion which the client may then either take up or ignore. All interventions are designed for the benefit of the client, to facilitate their work and help move them forwards. In co-counselling (in contrast to some more traditional ways of working) the purpose of an intervention is not to pursue the counsellor's own process or plan to resolve the client's problem.

An example of a co-counselling intervention is "What's On Top?". The question asks about what is foremost in conscious thought for the client, and is an invitation to articulate this without necessarily making sense. It is a useful way to start a session, especially when the client is not aware of any particular 'problem' they need to work on. Giving free reign to conscious thoughts gives the unconscious the chance to emerge. It helps the person to become present in the moment and to connect with their body and feelings.

For most students there is a tendency to focus on their ability to master the interventions as counsellor. Teachers will keep reminding them that the main task is in fact to learn to be a good client!

Indeed the whole emphasis of co-counselling is learning to work successfully on one's own material.

Intensive contract

In this type of contract the client indicates that they wish to work 'intensively'. This is the client's choice and also their responsibility. The difference for the counsellor is that they take *every* opportunity to offer an intervention. The skill of intensive working is not usually taught on fundamentals courses: most people come back to it once they have gained a bit of experience and feel more confident.

Safety

For co-counselling to be effective, we need to feel safe enough to trust it and use it to learn about ourselves. When we talk about things that are very personal to us, which often involve strong feelings, it is essential that we feel emotionally and physically safe.

The co-counselling model is built on a framework and culture that provides this support - although of course nothing in life is 100% safe. You may be invited to choose to stretch a boundary or to try things in a new way, and at all times you have the choice to accept or decline.

Safety within co-counselling is created in a number of ways. Firstly, everyone receives the same training, so each person knows what to expect and what to offer, regardless of what other training or experience they have. The training teaches each person how to listen well and build rapport within a session, so they can create a safe space for the client and also look after themselves when they are counsellor.

There are clear contracts and agreements that define a session. The principle of shared time is always adhered to. Interventions are specific and simple, which means you won't get invited to do something you don't understand or that is driven by the other person's agenda.

There are agreed ground rules, which include:

1. **No physical violence.** This means maintaining respect at all times for people, property and possessions. However distressed someone may be in the moment, they do not risk harm to other people, nor to buildings, property, fixtures and fittings.

Co-counselling is often done on the floor with cushions and mats, so that people can move around freely and maybe vent their feelings on soft things (like cushions) without risk of damage to themselves or anyone or anything else.

2. **Responsibility for self.** Co-counsellors are at all times aware of who they are and what they are doing, and take responsibility for it. In traditional one-way work it is the professional therapist or counsellor who is responsible for the session.

In co-counselling it is always *you* who is in charge and responsible for your session as client. A small part of yourself remains aware of what you are doing (this is a skill taught on the training, called maintaining your balance of attention).

Self-responsibility is also encouraged by getting people to use the word 'I' when talking about feelings, opinions or beliefs - rather than saying things like, "We want…" or "People say…" or "Everyone knows….". Being encouraged to change the pronoun to "I" focuses our attention on taking ownership for the statement rather than hiding behind generalisations, imagined restrictions or limiting beliefs.

3. **Confidentiality**. Your 'material' – whatever you work on during your session – is always owned solely by you. It may therefore not be referred to or used in any way by your counsellor outside of the session. That means it is not acceptable for your counsellor to carry on chatting about it afterwards; nor for them

to mention it to someone else. Nor is it OK for them to refer to it at any time in the future without your permission.

The same principle extends beyond pairs: anything shared in a co-counselling group is subject to the same rule of confidentiality. This is an important way of creating the feeling of safety: in this environment it is 'safe' to say whatever one needs to, knowing it will never be repeated unless the person who shared it chooses to raise it themselves.

4. **Non-judgemental.** Anything that is shared is accepted, allowed and heard without personal response or judgment from the counsellor. You may have a personal view (and emotional response) about what you hear, but within a session you learn how to put that aside and give the other person attention and acceptance in a way that is open, positive and non-judgemental.

5. **Quality of attention.** Co-counsellors choose not to co-counsel when under the influence of artificial mood changers such as drugs or alcohol. These substances impair the ability to be a fully attentive listener, and to be fully present in either role.

A prerequisite for undertaking a training in co-counselling is the potential ability to give good attention to the client when in the role of counsellor. If there is something big going on in a person's life that prevents them doing this it is often preferable for them to do some personal work (counselling or therapy) first.

What kind of things do people work on?

Sessions encompass the whole range of human issues - anything that upsets, worries or troubles people. They work on:

- Emotions they struggle to understand, to contain, or even to express.
- Problems with work, relationships, health, finances, sense of worth or meaning.
- Feelings they are dealing with right now, that are having a negative impact on their mind or body.
- Celebrating and sharing of exciting and positive things to increase their value.

9. How Are Sessions Used?

How often do people do sessions?

There's a lot of variety in timings... some people have regular and frequent sessions, others go for long periods without co-counselling until they have a particular need. Some set up an arrangement with a regular partner every week and may continue with it for years. Others do most of their work at residential events.

Some only arrange a session when they have a particular problem or something to celebrate. All these ways of working are fine: it's up to the individual and the speed at which they choose to work. The rule, as ever, is that the client is in charge of their process.

Where do co-counsellors hold their sessions?

Anywhere they feel safe and comfortable and feel able to express themselves freely. Most commonly that's in people's own homes, but also in rooms and centres that are hired for trainings, workshops or community days. And of course at residential events where typically either the whole venue is available or it provides dedicated space for co-counsellors only. The critical factors are to be able to work in safety and without interruption, and to preserve confidentiality for the people involved.

Some co-counsellors struggle to meet physically with others, or don't have many people nearby, or cannot get to events. Others simply find it hard to fit face-to-face session time into a busy schedule. In these cases, a helpful alternative may be to session on the phone.

Telephone co-counselling works surprisingly well for some people. Clearly there are significant differences - as you cannot see the person you are working with

- but the principles remain the same and it is quite possible to adapt the style to achieve a very satisfactory session.

Setting up a co-counselling session

One co-counsellor contacts another to ask for a session. If the second person agrees, they arrange a mutually suitable time and place to meet. As far as possible they arrange the environment to be comfortable and free from interruption or disturbance. They then agree the timings, and decide who will be client first. The first client specifies the contract they want and when they are ready, begins.

A sample co-counselling session

Here is an abbreviated example of opening dialogue from a session, with client and counsellor alternating (counsellor interventions are in bold). The client has asked for a normal contract:

(client sits in silence)

'What's on top?'

'Just having trouble settling down. Not sure what to talk about.' *(pause)*

'Actually I'm thinking about what just happened outside... I was a bit upset by what Jim said.....' *(tells the story)*

'What's the feeling?'

'Rather wobbly... shaky...'

'What else?'

'A bit of anxiety... I can feel some fear...'

'Where do you feel that?'

(placing hands) 'Here..... and here...' *(silence)*

'What's the thought?'

'I'm wondering why I let people upset me over such stupid things. He probably didn't mean any harm, it's just the way I react....' *(more exploration)*

'Is there something you want to say to Jim?'

'Yes.... I wish you would think a bit more before you speak. What seems like a harmless joke to you might actually be quite hurtful to other people...' *(a tear appears)*

'What's the feeling?'

'Sort of sad...' *(pause)*

'Have you felt like this before?'

'Yes... Quite often.'

'When was the first time?'

(scans memories) 'I can remember being quite young... and I was in the garden. My mother came outside and she....'

'Can you say it in the present tense?'

'OK... I'm in the garden... and I'm playing on the lawn.... my sister is there....' *(starts to give the detail of remembered experiences, including sounds, images, feelings, tastes etc. as if there now)*

'How old are you?'

'Not sure.... 6 I think, or 7 perhaps...' *(continues to recount the story)*

'What's the feeling?'

etc......

Commentary

This short extract of dialogue may have taken place over ten or fifteen minutes, with plenty of space for the client to think, feel and reflect, to scan their memory and recall particular incidents or examples of feelings. Sometimes things come to mind that the client does not understand or does not have words for. The counsellor encourages them (using co-counselling interventions only) to connect and express these things in movement, sounds or any way they choose, as this often leads to useful insights and actions.

All the while the counsellor is giving their full attention, and intervening when they sense it will help - for example to encourage the client to get more into their feelings, or to express what is not being said. The intention always is to assist, facilitate and support. The client is always free to pick up the suggestion or to ignore it if it doesn't feel helpful or appropriate.

Action Setting

Action setting is a co-counselling intervention which may be offered or requested towards the end of a session. It is an optional but often valuable part of the work of re-evaluation... learning from the past, while being in the present, in order to change the future.

When you have gained new understanding from exploring and expressing emotions, it is often helpful to consolidate the learning by identifying specific things you plan to do. Naturally not every piece of work needs to end with identifying actions, as it depends on the purpose of the session.

After a session it's possible to feel really clear and know exactly what's going to be different and how you are going to make it happen: then you get home and find you've forgotten it all. An action plan can capture your thinking at the time so you can carry on working with it later.

Example 1 – In exploring a problem you are having with someone at work, you realise you are being negatively affected because they strongly remind you of someone from your past. In this case the realisation itself may be all that's needed for the feelings to dissipate and the issue to fade away.

Example 2 - You have a problem with a tough decision at work that is prompting strong feelings. After exploring the situation in a co-counselling session you feel much better and more resourceful. Now you want to use the insights to generate some specific actions to change your behaviour and plan what you will do in the next week or two.

In the second example, you might ask your counsellor to do some Action Setting with you. They ask questions to help you identify the specifics of what you want to achieve and what steps are involved. The questions help you identify whether you have enough clarity and insight to move forward and make a specific plan or whether you need to do some more emotional work. Once the emotions are expressed, it is much easier to think clearly and creatively about solutions and create a plan on which you can successfully follow through.

There can be continuity in co-counselling when people work on an issue over time. An action plan may be written down and brought to a follow-up session. It can be easy to neglect action setting and overlook its importance... but if we do co-counselling in order to live happier and more effective lives, we need to take the learnings from our past into our future.

Action setting is a positive way to achieve this – to create change and prevent 'navel-contemplation'. It is a central part of the CCI model as developed by John Heron.

Overall structure of a co-counselling session

This is the outline structure of a session:

Agree session length and who goes first

- Agree type of contract, and timing
- Do first person's session
- Optional **Action Setting***
- Offer ending interventions like **Nutshell** * or **Celebration** *
- Offer **Attention Switch** *

Change Over

- Agree type of contract, and timing
- Do second person's session
- Optional Action Setting
- Offer Nutshell, Celebration
- Offer Attention Switch

Feedback * as both client and counsellor

End of session.

* These are examples of interventions.

Nutshell is an invitation to summarise the session in a sentence or two, to clarify insights.

Celebration ('What can you celebrate about your session, and yourself?') encourages personal changes, increases empowerment and internal support.

Attention Switch helps the client to 'come back to normal' so they are ready to change over and become the counsellor.

Feedback encourages self-learning about how your client and counsellor skills are developing. Note that the counsellor never gives feedback on the performance of the client.

Action Setting is described above.

"People take different roads seeking fulfillment and happiness. Just because they're not on your road doesn't mean they've gotten lost."

– *H. Jackson Brown*

10. Where Did It Come From?

Brief origins of CCI

Co-counselling has been around for 40 years or so. It was originally developed in America by **Harvey Jackins**, the founder and principal theorist of Re-evaluation Counseling (RC). Building on the theory of Dianetics (invented by L. Ron Hubbard) in the 1950s, Jackins developed the theory that human beings could substantially improve their lives and emotional well-being through the systematic process of 'discharge' (crying, laughing, yawning etc). He came to believe that this would be actively encouraged by the mutual exchange of aware attention... which became the co-counselling process.

John Heron was in the 1970s founder and director of the Human Potential Research Project at the University of Surrey: the first university-based centre for humanistic and transpersonal psychology and education in Europe. He was a leading facilitator and trainer in many fields, including co-operative inquiry, personal and transpersonal development, group facilitation and interactive skills, professional development in medicine, psychotherapy and the helping professions... and co-counselling.

In 1974 John Heron broke away from the Harvey Jackins group, feeling that that since co-counselling is based on equality, it needed a less hierarchical organisation. He, with others, created Co-Counselling International (CCI) as a peer network.

Note: If you are interested in the background and theoretical development of co-counselling, there's a short summary in 'Further Information'.

How is CCI run?

In the UK, CCI is a 'flat' organisation with no hierarchy, which means there is no single person or body in charge. Everyone has a say and a stake in what happens, and shares responsibility for decision-making processes. Co-counselling is an organic and flowing community formed of the group of people that come together within it at any given time. The organisation has no continuing independent existence, rather it is at any stage defined by its current active participants. This can be seen as both its strength and its weakness.

CCI is made up of networks of large and small groups with communities in Australia, Belgium, England, Germany, Hungary, Ireland, Netherlands, Scotland, USA and New Zealand. Each country has its own structures and decision-making processes, and its own regional communities. Throughout the life of co-counselling, its international gatherings have drawn large numbers of participants from many countries – a prime example of successfully combining autonomy and collaboration.

Community activity

These are the kind of things a local or regional co-counselling community might do:

- Maintain a contact list so that people can get in touch with each other.
- Run planned or informal events, such as community days or evenings, where people can meet to have sessions, work in groups, learn or practise new ideas in workshops.
- Offer day or residential events for the wider community and invite people from outside the area.
- Co-operate with other groups to run national or even international residential events.

UK CCI residentials are wide-ranging in scope, numbers and locations. There are weekends for relatively small numbers (10 to 15), and a variety of ong weekends' for 30 to 50 people. These take place in venues around England and Scotland. Each year there are also one or two international events in any of the host countries, which may attract 100 or more people.

Communities online

As you would expect in the 21st century, there is a thriving virtual community based around email and the internet, using websites and social media. The primary **email** communication network is a closed group known as 'cocolist', which provides a way for co-counsellors to make contact, together with a forum for discussion, questions, news and announcements.

Presently there are two UK **newsletters**, one paper-based and one electronic. Several local communities also publish newsletters as a way of keeping people involved with what's going on.

There are also a number of co-counselling **websites**, most of which have public areas as well as those available only to accredited co-counsellors. These are listed in 'Further Information'.

11. Personal Experiences

Here are some examples of what people have gained from their co-counselling experience, told in their own words:

"Through co-counselling, I have grown in confidence in expressing my opinions, my needs, my feelings and my boundaries. Co-counselling has also helped me 'lighten up' – as I've shed a lot of my unhealthy rules and restrictions, I have found a huge capacity for spontaneous fun, creativity and playfulness."
Sarah, Age 41, UK

"I really value the contact with people who have learnt to be in touch with their truth. I also value the sense of fun and creativity which is an essential part

of becoming my true self and is really enjoyable."
Judy, Age 53, Academic, UK

"Through co-counselling I have discovered how much energy I actually have." *Till, Age 41 Male. Teacher, Germany*

"Attending Co-Counselling Training has changed my life! It has helped me to find a confidence and an acceptance of myself that I did not know I felt. I have learnt to know my strengths and weaknesses with greater awareness. It has taught me how to manage conflict." *K, Age 52. Female. Therapist, UK*

"I learned so much about my own feelings - that I could handle them much better. I still use sessions to discharge, but for me it is now more important to use the time of a session to focus on the future and make concrete action plans... Therefore I have the idea to be much more successful in my life!"
Sytse, Age 62. Male. Teacher. Netherlands

"I discovered co-counselling at a time when I was very unhappy and had little or nothing in the way of personal support. It was a relief to find a place safe enough to begin to allow out some of the feelings that had been suppressed for many years. Over the years co-co has been a vital part of my growth and development, complementing other effective ways of working." *Steve, Age 56. UK*

"When my mother died I got a lot of support from my co-counselling, it allowed me in a role-play to get out all my anger which helped me a lot." *Cornelia, Age 31. Education, Germany*

"A friend recommended co-counselling to me, I was in total despair and misery at the time of the breakdown of my second marriage (the first had ended in an acrimonious divorce). Co-Counselling gave me the space to grieve, and the tools to begin to process my hurt, grief, and anger." *Virginia, Age 70. Civil Servant, Scotland*

"Co-counselling taught me many skills that I use regularly at work… and in all aspects of my life."
Sue, Age 51. Programme Manager, UK

"I come from a family where the habit is to bottle everything up and carry on until we break down, or turn to drink to suppress our feelings. Through co-counselling I have learned how to let my feelings out, to cry, laugh, scream, shake, yawn, shout, or whatever I need to do, within a session. After a session I can carry on thinking and functioning so much better, even when life is tough. It is my ongoing practice to keep in good health."
Kate, Age 40. Administrator, UK

"Co-counselling has given me back a sense of who I am." *Mark, Age 47. Health Worker, UK*

"Co-Counselling sessions clarify and verify my thinking. Clarify means that I can distinguish better between more or less important matters for me."
Rudolf G, Age 59. Engineer, Germany

"Over 10 years ago when my children were quite young, I realized I had to find a better way to deal with my feelings of frustration and anger. I knew it was completely unfair and quite destructive to react to my children's needs through my distress. I began to search for help and found co-counselling.

Now my children know that I believe in them, that their mother knows they are brilliant, capable and very special individuals... I have learned to listen to myself, to those around me and to cherish and celebrate life."

Janice, Age 45. Researcher, Israel

"Every single Human Being at every moment of the past - if the entire situation is taken into account - has always done the very best he or she could do, and so deserves neither blame nor reproach from anyone including self. This in particular is true for you."

- *Harvey Jackins*

12. Conclusion

Summary

By now we hope you will be clear about what co-counselling is, why people do it, and what they get from it. You should also have a feel for how it works... what happens in trainings, in sessions, and in the wider communities.

To summarise, co-counselling is:

- Completely free after the initial training.
- An equal exchange of time, skills and attention.
- Self-directed: the client is always in charge of their own work.
- A lifelong system of personal and emotional support.

- A method for building and maintaining emotional intelligence.
- A way to create a network of friends, colleagues and supporters.

What Next?

1. If you are interested in learning co-counselling (for yourself or friends or a team at work), use the websites to find a teacher in your area. Contact them for information and to find out about plans for tasters and Fundamentals trainings. If there is no teacher listed, invite one to your area or talk to the contact person listed for your county.

2. We are very interested in your feedback on this book. Please let us know... did it answer your questions, was it clear, was it helpful, was anything missing? Your comments, suggestions and queries are all welcome (See Section 16.)

13. Further Information

Websites

The CCI (UK) website provides much useful information, including details of trainings and teachers: www.co-counselling.org.uk.

Other helpful co-counselling websites include:

    www.cocoscotland.co.uk

    www.co-cornucopia.org.uk

    www.londoncocounselling.fsnet.co.uk

    www.cciwns.com.

Recommended Reading

From the multitude of related books, these six are for the authors significant and relevant to the co-counselling way of thinking and working:

"Time to Think" – *Nancy Kline*

"The Power of Now" – *Eckhart Tolle*

"The Endorphin Effect" – *William Bloom*

"Man's Search For Meaning" – *Viktor Frankl*

"Helping the Client: A Creative Practical Guide"
    – *John Heron*

"Emotional Intelligence: Why it Can Matter
    More Than IQ" – *Daniel Goleman*

Models and Concepts

The ideas and techniques used in co-counselling are drawn from a number of other commonly used psychodynamic principles and models. For example:

Person-Centered Therapy (and the Humanistic school of psychotherapies) - aims to help clients achieve a stronger and more healthy sense of self, and a belief in their capacity for self-direction and understanding of their own development. Psychologists in this area include *Carl Rogers, B.F. Skinner, Abraham Maslow, Erik Erikson, Carl Jung.*

Catharsis – (meaning cleansing or purging) is a release of emotional tension. Experiencing and expressing the deep emotions often associated with events in the individual's past which were originally repressed or ignored, leads to healing and integration. This is an idea from Freudian psychoanalysis.

Primal Therapy – is a trauma-based psychotherapy created by Arthur Janov, which suggests that neurosis is caused by the repressed pain of childhood trauma. Janov believes the repressed pain can be brought to conscious awareness and resolved through re-experiencing the incident and fully expressing the resulting pain during therapy. *Arthur Janov, Michael Holden*.

Gestalt – is an experiential form of psychotherapy that emphasises personal responsibility. It focuses on the individual's experience in the present moment and the self-regulating adjustments made as a result of experience. The German term *gestalt* refers to how a thing has been 'put together' and is often translated as 'pattern' in psychology. The phrase "the whole is greater than the sum of the parts" is often used when explaining Gestalt theory.

Body-Orientated Psychotherapy – addresses the importance of the body and the mind as a whole, and the complex reciprocal relationships between body and mind. The concepts of 'energy' in the body are similar to energy concepts of Eastern medicines and philosophies such as yoga, acupuncture, and tai chi. *Wilhelm Reich, Pierre Janet, Sigmund Freud*.

Transference – is the unconscious assignment to others of feelings and attitudes associated with significant figures from early life. Treating your boyfriend as if he were your Dad is an example of how someone might transfer feelings about a figure from the past onto a person in current life. This is a concept initially developed by Freud.

14. FAQs

Answers to some Frequently Asked Questions:

What IS co-counselling?

It's a method for increasing emotional intelligence and stimulating individual growth. It's a network of like-minded people who offer each other a personal and emotional support system. It's a way to express and manage your difficult feelings and to learn more about yourself.

What's the difference between CCI and RC?

Both organisations teach and use co-counselling, but within different structures and belief systems. This book is about CCI. An internet search will reveal a wealth of information about RC.

- **How does it differ from ordinary counselling?**
  It is based on an equal exchange of time and skills. No money changes hands. Nobody is an expert: everyone undergoes the same training.

- **Why does it have this name?**
  It is a joint, shared, and equal activity ('co'), based on a form of 'counselling'. The name can be a drawback, as many people assume it is just another form of standard professional counselling. It might be more accurately called 'co-listening'.

- **Who is in charge, who makes the decisions, who takes responsibility?**
  CCI is a peer organisation, so no individual or body is in charge. There is a collective responsibility for everything that happens.

- **Is co-counselling relevant in the workplace?**
  Absolutely. It has successfully been introduced in organisations under the name of 'professional partnering' or 'peer staff support'. Contact the authors if you want to know more.

- **Why is it not more widely known and used?**

  Its growth depends on individuals spreading the word. Many people are content to use it for themselves without putting effort into recruiting others. There is no central body to co-ordinate publicity and marketing.

- **How do I find out if there is co-counselling activity in my area?**

  Look at the websites and talk to your local contact person. Once trained, if there is nobody nearby, try phone co-counselling, make contacts at residentials, ask a teacher to run a training in your area.

- **Can I do co-counselling with my friends, or with my partner?**

  Opinion differs. Some people like to keep things separate, so they can session with people they don't know socially. Others like to combine the two, finding it possible to maintain the boundaries even to the extent of doing sessions with their life partner. It's a choice for you to make.

- **What is the typical age range for co-counselling?**

  Anywhere between 20 and 90: most are probably in their 40s and 50s. It seems to appeal to people after they have had some life experience.

- **What do you mean by 'work' or 'material'?**

  It's the actual content of your session, the things you want to talk about. There may be issues that cause you problems or difficulties in your life, or you may need to make a tough decision, or you want to explore something, or to celebrate challenges you've overcome.

  Often in a session we want to resume a former piece of work, something from our inner world that is part of ongoing personal growth. Anything that an individual works on in sessions is regarded as their 'material', and is not to be referred to by others without permission.

15. Glossary

Accreditation
A peer process at the end of Fundamentals which assesses a person's suitability to become a co-counsellor and join the community.

Action Setting
A set of interventions in a co-counselling session in which the client transfers new understanding and insights from their inner world to their outer world, by identifying specific actions to create or consolidate change.

Balance of Attention
The ability to maintain a part of yourself in awareness of who you are now and what you are doing. This is a skill that is taught on Fundamentals training.

Behavioural Flexibility
Being open-minded and able to recognise the validity of new or differing views. Adapting behaviour as necessary to suit the situation. Flexibility of behaviour increases

our ability to be successful in the world.

Belief

A generalisation about the state of the world or our ability to act in the world. It may or may not actually be true, and may or may not be helpful to us. Though beliefs drive our behaviour, many are out of our conscious awareness.

Catharsis

The relieving of anxiety by bringing repressed feelings and fears into consciousness. The releasing of emotional tension, often after a significant experience, that restores or refreshes the spirit.

Celebration

A co-counselling intervention that draws our conscious attention to that which we choose to recognise, validate and honour in ourselves and our actions.

CCI

Co-Counselling International. The network of individuals and groups engaged in the John Heron version of co-counselling.

Client

The co-counsellor who is taking their turn at working on their chosen issues within a session.

Co-counselling	A method for promoting and maintaining optimal mental health, and increasing emotional intelligence. A community of trained co-counsellors.
Contract	The agreement defining and supporting a co-counselling session. May be free attention, normal or intensive.
Counsellor	The co-counsellor who is taking their turn within a session to listen to the client and to offer free attention or interventions.
Discharge	The pouring forth or releasing of strong feelings; the act of venting; the sudden giving off of energy.
Emotion	An internal experience which arises spontaneously rather than through conscious effort, and which is often accompanied by physiological changes.
Emotional Intelligence	The awareness of and ability to manage one's emotions in a healthy and productive way. A high EQ is thought to be more important in many walks of life than a high IQ.

Free Attention	A co-counselling contract. High quality listening that is free from comment, interpretation or input of any kind from the listener.
Framework	System provided by co-counselling based on the session structure, plus interventions, principles, ground rules and culture.
Fundamentals	The training course that teaches the basic skills of co-counselling, and which is the pre-requisite for accreditation as a co-counsellor and for entry into CCI.
Intervention	Words or gestures offered during a session by the person currently in the role of counsellor, designed to facilitate the client in their work.
Nutshell	A co-counselling intervention that invites us to briefly summarise our session to clarify insights.
Pattern	A repetitive piece of behaviour that is out of awareness and rooted in the past, where an old stimulus triggers a predictable response which is often unhelpful in the present.

Re-evaluation   Looking at things differently after discharge and catharsis. Putting a different interpretation or meaning on past events, thereby allowing new ways of being in the future.

RC   Re-evaluation Counselling. The network of individuals and groups engaged in the Harvey Jackins version of co-counselling.

Session   The formal exchange of equal time and skills that takes place between two co-counsellors who have agreed to work together.

Self-esteem   The overall evaluation or appraisal of one's own worth. Self-esteem may be reflected in behaviour - such as assertiveness, shyness, confidence or caution.

Taster   A short event offered by teachers of co-counselling, designed to give people an initial experience to see if it works for them.

Value   A concept that is important to us, like freedom, respect, or equality. Though our personal values often drive our behaviour, many are out of our awareness.

Unconscious The part of our mind that is not in our awareness, which is estimated to be in excess of 85%. Also known as the subconscious.

16. The Authors

Steve Roche

Steve has trained in a wide range of models and systems over several decades in the self-help business. He discovered co-counselling as a powerful agent for change in the early 90s, and believes the skills it teaches to be among the most valuable he has learned for both professional practice and personal life. Steve is a writer and trainer, and a professional life coach specialising in applied NLP. He owns a company called Personal Transformations.

Sue Gray

Sue has been a co-counsellor for over 20 years and a teacher of co-counselling for the past ten. It was one of the first self-development tools she discovered and it transformed her life both at home and at work. She believes the skills co-counselling teaches are relevant in all parts of her life then and now. Sue has also taught co-counselling as a staff support system in health and social care settings. She works as a Project Manager for a charity.

Sue and Steve both trained as co-counselling teachers with Gretchen Pyves in 1998. They run co-counselling workshops and residential events and teach regular Fundamentals courses in Suffolk.

For information about trainings in Suffolk, and also about co-counselling at work, see

www.suffolk-coaching.com

To contact us, please email
steve.roche@btinternet.com

or contactsue@yahoo.co.uk.

"You are led through your lifetime by the inner learning creature, the playful spiritual being that is your real self.

Don't turn away from possible futures before you are certain you don't have anything to learn from them.
You're always free to choose a different future, or a different past."

from "Illusions: The Adventures of a Reluctant Messiah"

by Richard Bach